Time Detectives

Written by Robyn O'Sullivan
Series Consultant: Linda Hoyt

WorldWise
Content-based Learning

Contents

Chapter 1

Puzzles of the past

Detectives find out information and try to solve puzzles. Crime detectives look for evidence of what happened, and to do this they ask questions, examine the crime scene and use technology.

Did you know there's another kind of detective? Time detectives solve the puzzles of the past. They find information about life on Earth – who and what lived where and when. You might wonder how time detectives can find information about things that happened thousands or millions of years ago.

Palaeontologists are time detectives. They study **fossils** to find out about the history of life on Earth. The most common fossils are bones, shells and imprints. An imprint might be a footprint or the outline of an animal or plant on rock or wood.

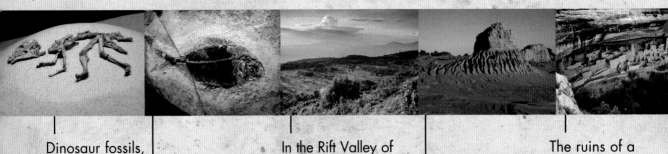

Dinosaur fossils, 560 million years old, were found in Australia.

Dinosaur fossils (Hypsilophodon), 120 million years old, were found in the United Kingdom.

In the Rift Valley of Africa, archaeologists found human fossils that are three million years old.

At Lake Mungo in Australia, archaeologists found human bones that are about 40,000 years old.

The ruins of a Puebloan culture reveal the existence of the Anasazi people, who lived around the Four Corners area, near Utah, in the United States, about 10,000 years ago.

Archaeologists are time detectives too. They study human remains and the things people made to find out how people lived. The objects that have been made by humans are called artefacts.

Time detectives have solved many puzzles from the past. This timeline shows some places where archaeologists and palaeontologists have studied artefacts and fossils to learn about who or what lived in these places.

Stonehenge is a **prehistoric** monument in the United Kingdom that was created over 4,000 years ago.

Pompeii is a town that was buried by volcanic ash in 79 CE. Archaeologists study the artifacts found at Pompeii to learn about the people who lived there.

The Egyptian pyramids are about 5,000 years old. They contain information about the **ancient** Egyptian way of life.

In 1974, over 8,000 life-size statues were found buried in an emperor's **tomb** in China. These statues are about 2,200 years old.

Machu Picchu was an Incan city over 600 years ago. Archaeologists learn about who lived there by examining the ruins of the city.

Chapter 2

Fossil fever

The earth's crust is full of buried treasures, such as gold and oil, that are worth a lot of money. **Fossils** are important treasures too – not because they are worth money, but because they reveal secrets about past life on Earth. Fossils show the shapes and sizes of many animals and plants that have lived on Earth. When scientists study fossils, they learn what these animals and plants looked like, as well as where and when they lived. Without fossils, we would never have found out about dinosaurs.

Time detectives at work

Palaeontologists solved the puzzle of how the Hypsilophodon (say: hip-see-low-foe-don) dinosaur moved around when they examined Hypsilophodon bone fossils. For about 100 years, palaeontologists thought the Hypsilophodon dinosaur had the ability to climb trees. When they took a closer look at the bones they learned that this dinosaur could not climb trees, because the bones in its feet were the wrong shape for climbing.

Interview with a palaeontologist

Our reporter Annette Twain speaks to palaeontologist Gabriel Cruz about the discovery of some dinosaur fossils.

Q. What are you doing?

A. We are looking for the fossils of a dinosaur that lived around 120 million years ago. We have set up a **dig** where fossils have already been found – and we have discovered more fossils.

Q. What did you do after you found the dinosaur bones?

A. After we found the dinosaur bones, we used hammers and chisels to loosen the surrounding rock and soil. We used dental picks to lift out the bones and soft brushes to remove the soil. We kept notes, drew diagrams and took photographs of everything we did.

Q. Did you rebuild the dinosaur?

A. Yes, we took all our fossils back to the laboratory, where we cleaned them. It took a long time because we had to be so careful not to damage them. Finally we put the bones together. We studied other fossil skeletons to help us figure out where the bones should go.

Q. How did you know what the dinosaur would have looked like when it was alive?

A. When the skeleton was put together, some other experts made predictions about how the dinosaurs would have looked. Marks on the bones showed where the muscles would have been and how big they were. When these experts study the features of related animals such as birds, which have many similar body features to dinosaurs, and lizards, which, like dinosaurs, are reptiles, they can make predictions about how the dinosaurs might have looked.

Australian dinosaur fossils

The Australian Dinosaur Museum near Winston in Queensland has the biggest collection of Australia's largest dinosaur fossils. Paleontologists show visitors how to prepare dinosaur fossils ready for scientific study and display.

Be a time detective

Scientists cannot tell from fossils what colours the dinosaurs were. When faced with a puzzle like this, scientists brainstorm possible solutions, then test their ideas.

Choose a type of dinosaur and find out where it lived and what type of body covering it would have had. Use this information to choose the colour you think it might have been.

A model of an ankylosaur

Canadian fossil discovery
Ping Pong ichthyosaurs

Fossils that were 100 million years old were found under a ping-pong table in a science laboratory at the University of Alberta in Canada. Dr Michael Caldwell made the discovery when he was clearing out the lab for renovations. Students had dug up the fossils 25 years earlier and stored them in boxes under the table. It seems the bones had been forgotten.

The fossils were the bones of ichthyosaurs (say: *ik-thee-oh-sawrs*), which were dolphin-shaped sea creatures that lived during the time of dinosaurs. Palaeontologists discovered that one of the creatures was pregnant with two babies. This proves that ichthyosaurs did not lay eggs but gave birth to live babies.

This is what palaeontologists think the ichthyosaur might have looked like.

Chapter 3

Ancient Egypt

In **ancient** times, Egypt was the richest and most powerful country in the world. The ancient Egyptian **civilisation** lasted for about 3,500 years.

Fantastic pharaohs

Egyptian kings were called pharaohs. They built enormous **tombs** for when they died – these tombs are called pyramids. The pyramids had many rooms that were filled with everything the pharaoh would need for the afterlife. In the heart of the pyramid was a special room lined with gold where the pharaoh was buried.

Afterlife beliefs

- Ancient Egyptians believed that after you died, you had another life – the afterlife.
- They believed that to have an afterlife, the dead person's heart must be full of goodness. The heart was weighed by the Goddess Ma'at on the scales of truth and justice. If the person had led a good life, their heart would weigh less than the goddess's feather, and they could go on to the afterlife.
- People had to take everything with them to the afterlife, so their tombs were filled with all the things needed for living, as well as tools for working.

Buried treasures

Items found in ancient Egyptian pyramids included:
- wooden and ivory toys
- board games
- dice carved from stone or ivory
- harps and flutes
- food
- gold, silver and jewellery
- boats and tools
- statues of slaves and animals
- clothes, wigs, perfume and makeup

Archaeologists know how the pharaohs looked from studying the pictures on the walls inside the pyramids. The pharaohs in these pictures wore shoes made of gold, and crowns that were 30 centimetres high. Some wore white clothes with huge jewelled collars, and some had cones of wax on their hair and bold makeup on their eyes.

Time detectives at work

Archaeologists solved many puzzles about daily life in ancient Egypt when they examined pyramids in Egypt. The pyramids revealed what ancient Egyptians ate, the games they played, how they dressed and many other aspects of ancient Egyptian life.

Write your name in hieroglyphs

The ancient Egyptians invented a form of picture writing called hieroglyphics.

Use the table below to write your name in Egyptian hieroglyphs.

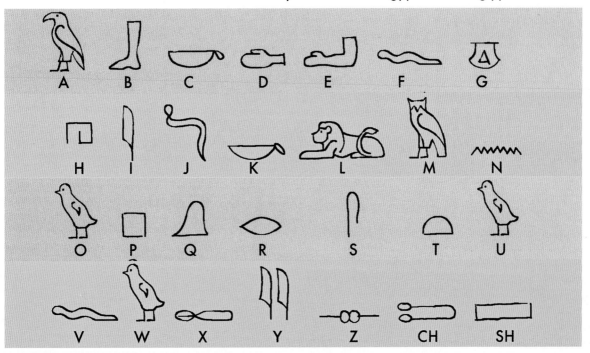

Secrets of a civilisation

A report by archaeology student, Shane Cobb

The discovery of the tombs inside the pyramids revealed information about the ancient Egyptian way of living. The tombs were filled with everyday items that the pharaohs used, as well as chariots and boats that the pharaohs needed for transportation. There were statues of servants to do the pharaoh's work in the afterlife, and tools and household items that they needed. Paintings of daily life on the tomb walls showed people farming the land, boats on the Nile River, and people playing music and dancing. From looking inside the tombs, archaeologists discovered many facts about how people lived and worked in ancient Egypt.

This painting of workers dragging building blocks dates from 1,000 BCE.

Detail from carvings on the tomb walls

Archaeologists are still unsure about how the pyramids were built. Some experts think that a ramp was built up to the base of the pyramid and extended as the pyramid was built. The workers might have pulled the huge blocks to the ramp on rollers, then up the ramp on sleds. They probably used **papyrus** ropes, pulleys and levers to lift the blocks of stone into position. It is remarkable that these huge structures could have been built without modern machinery.

Great Pyramid facts

The Great Pyramid of Giza is the largest pyramid in Egypt. Experts can't say exactly how many years it took to build, or how many workers were needed. Here are some estimates.

Built: About 4,500 years ago

Height: At the time of construction it was 147 metres

Number of blocks used: Approximately 2,300,000

Weight of blocks: Most weighed between two and four tonnes, but some were as much as 80 tonnes

Number of workers: Anywhere from 30,000–100,000

What they used: Tools such as levers, ramps, rollers and pulleys

The birth of maths

Egyptians calculate

By studying the ancient Egyptian number system, we know that the ancient Egyptians had ways of calculating numbers. They used **algebra** and **geometry** to figure out how to build the pyramids. They could also add and subtract, but they couldn't multiply because their number system didn't have a zero. So, how can you do maths without a zero? You can use pictures to represent numbers. Here's how the ancient Egyptians did it.

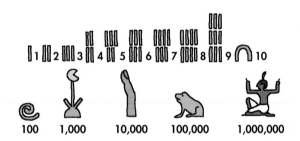

Figure it out

Can you solve this maths problem for the pharaoh's chief builder and choose the Egyptian answer?

The pharaoh wants  statues built for his pyramid.

It takes the workers days to build each statue. The builder needs to calculate how many days it will take to build all the statues. Which answer is correct (see answer below)?

A

B

The answer is B.

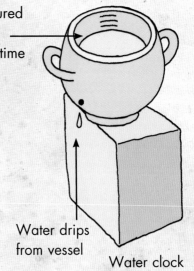

Water level measured against marks to count the passing time

Water drips from vessel

Water clock

Telling time

The discovery of **sundials** and **obelisks** in the ruins of ancient Egypt show us that the ancient Egyptians used these instruments to tell the time. They knew what the time was by watching the movement of the shadow from the sun. This worked well when the sun was shining but not on cloudy days or at night. They solved this problem by inventing the water clock. This was a stone container that had a line of marks on the inside. The container was filled with water, which dripped out slowly through a hole at the bottom. As the water level dropped the marks were exposed, showing how much time had passed.

The ancient Egyptians also invented the first calendar with 365 days in the year. Their calendar was based on the cycle of the Nile River, which flooded at the same time each year.

At first the ancient Egyptians didn't have a leap year. But after 1,000 years they realised there were 250 days in their calendar not accounted for. They figured out that if they added an extra day to the calendar every fourth year, there wouldn't be any days left over.

Find out more

Find out how many:
• days per week
• weeks per month
• months per season
• seasons per year
there were in the ancient Egyptian calendar.

Chapter 4

Pompeii unearthed

In the year 79 CE, a volcano in Italy called Mount Vesuvius erupted. Hot ash and rocks rained down on the nearby city of Pompeii, completely covering it, and it remained buried for more than 1,650 years, until the year 1730.

A street in Pompeii

Time detectives at work

Archaeologists are still **excavating** the area around Pompeii. They find art, **architecture** and artefacts that help solve puzzles about **ancient Roman** customs, such as how the Romans cooked, what they ate, what clothes they wore and what they did for entertainment.

A moment in time

At the time of the eruption of Vesuvius, Pompeii was a busy city. It was a port, a market for local produce, a business centre, and a resort for wealthy Romans. An oval-shaped wall with seven gates surrounded the city. Important buildings surrounded a central square called the Forum.

Pompeii, with Mount Vesuvius looming in the distance

The eruption of the volcano was so violent and swift that many people were unable to escape. Some were trapped in their homes. Many people were hit by flying rocks and **debris**. Others died from the poisonous fumes that spread across the land.

When Mount Vesuvius erupted, hot ash poured over people and then set as it cooled and dried. Over time, the people's bodies **decomposed**, leaving an empty mould. When archaeologists filled the moulds with clay, it was like re-forming the bodies. The archaeologists could see what the people looked like, the clothes they were wearing and the expressions on their faces when they died.

Archaeologists have made many discoveries while excavating Pompeii. The ruins, artefacts and **fossils** show how the people lived. Archaeologists believe most homes had more than one storey, and the rooms were grouped around a visitors' room called an atrium. Some homes had shops at street level.

Sofia

A visit to Pompeii

Last year, Sofia took a holiday with her uncle in Naples. She wrote a letter to her parents.

Dear Mum and Dad,

Uncle Gino took me to Pompeii. It was fantastic. We walked along cobbled streets and I could see the ruts made by the wheels of chariots 2,000 years ago!

I saw how archaeologists had scraped away soil from old pieces of pottery. They used little brushes and worked very carefully. The tour guide told me that Pompeii was buried under ash after Vesuvius erupted.

Tourists in the amphitheatre arena at Pompeii

It was rediscovered almost 300 years ago. Since then three-quarters of the city has been uncovered.

My favourite place was the Forum Baths, which were public baths.

In one room there were glass cases with plaster casts of real people who had died during the eruption. You can see the look of pain and horror on their faces. It's gruesome!

The gladiator cells near the theatre are gruesome too. Gladiators were slaves and prisoners of war who had to entertain the people by fighting each other until one of them died. Some of the gladiators were really popular – just like sports stars.

Plaster casts from Pompeii

Later in the day I saw the remains of a food shop that sold fast food! I wonder if they sold pizza? There was a bakery too. It's amazing that some things are still the same today as they were so long ago!

See you soon.
Love, Sofia

Old bread recovered
from the Pompeii ruins

Pompeii, then and now

The illustrations below show a bakery, a food shop and the Forum Baths as they would have looked before the volcanic eruption of Mount Vesuvius. The photographs show us how they look now – almost 2,000 years after the buildings were covered in hot ash from the volcano.

... then

... now

▶ The remains of this Roman bakery show the wood-fired oven and the millstones that were used to make flour. As the grain was poured into the funnel-shaped stone, the stone was rotated by hand, or possibly by donkey, and crushed against the bottom stone to make flour.

▼ The remains of this Roman food shop show containers sunk into a stone counter. These were thought to have contained hot food that was sold to customers. In the remains of one food shop, more than a thousand coins were found. These shops may have been more like restaurants or modern-day cafes and bars. Experts think they were decorated with paintings and sculptures.

▼ The Forum Baths were one of the bath complexes in Pompeii. There were separate sections for men and women. The bath complexes contained dressing rooms, and hot, cold and warm baths, as well as public areas such as gardens and open spaces where people could gather together.

Chapter 5

The Anasazi people

Anasazi houses built into the cliff

Four corners in the USA is where four states meet: Utah, Colorado, Arizona and New Mexico

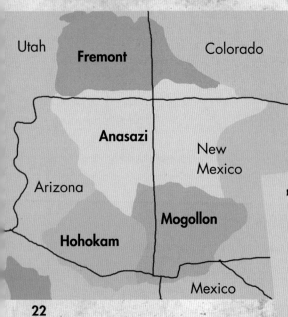

Thousands of years ago, the Anasazi people lived in the area that is now the southwestern United States. This area was known as the Four Corners.

The ways of the ancestors

Long, long ago, a tribe of **nomads** wandered in the lands called the Four Corners. The men hunted large animals. The women gathered wild plants for grinding into flour. They put hot stones from the fire straight into baskets of food to cook it.

The children gathered wood for the fires, and learned the ways of their elders. The people wore clothes made of fur or turkey feathers, and plaited or woven sandals. They sheltered in caves. They took part in running sports and played games using small discs.

Time detectives at work

Experts have examined the ruined dwellings of the Anasazi people. This has helped them to solve the puzzle of what the Anasazi traditions and beliefs were.

Anasazi ruins in Arizona

Time passed and the people settled in one place. They began to grow corn for grinding into flour. Then they grew other crops such as beans and squash. They stored their food in the caves and built houses dug into the ground, known as pit houses. The women were amazing basket weavers. They made baskets for many uses, including cooking and carrying water.

Building a pit house

The Anasazi people built pit houses to live in. They dug a pit in the ground and built a fireplace in the middle. They built walls around the pit with stones or logs stacked on top of each other. The walls narrowed at the top and were covered with a roof made from sticks and mud. There was a hole in the centre of the roof to let out smoke from the fire. The people put a ladder up through the hole to get in and out of the house.

Over time, the people moved to the Chaco Canyon, in New Mexico, to build a new settlement. They built houses with sandstone and wood. The houses had many storeys. Some of them had as many as 100 rooms.

From the central settlement, the people built roads to outlying villages. The people farmed the land and made pottery as well as baskets. They traded goods among themselves and with other tribes. The people prospered, and their leaders were rich and powerful.

Eventually the Chaco Canyon settlement failed (see "Puzzles of Chaco Canyon" on page 25). The people scattered to different parts of the land. Some call these people the Anasazi. Others call them the Ancestral Puebloans, while still others know them as the Hisat-Sinom.

Ruins of Anasazi dwellings

Puzzles of Chaco Canyon

There are many unsolved puzzles about the people who lived at Chaco Canyon.
Archaeologists have thought of some possible solutions to the puzzles.
What do you think?

Why were the people nomads?

- They had to find food so they followed herds of animals.

Why did the people stop being nomads?

- They found a place where the animals and plants were plentiful.
- They began to grow crops and no longer needed to travel in search of food.

Why did the people move to Chaco Canyon?

- There was a long spell of drought.
- Warrior tribes, such as the Apache and the Navajo, arrived in the old area where the Anasazi had been living.

Why did the settlement have roads?

- Food could easily be transported to people who needed it.
- The people could make **pilgrimages** to the central canyon for spiritual reasons.
- The central settlement was a centre for agriculture, the making of crafts, and trade.
- Roads showed that the leaders were powerful and wealthy.

Why did the people leave Chaco Canyon?

- There was not enough water.
- There were too many people.
- The people had used up the natural resources.

ARCHAEOLOGICAL DIG AT CHACO CANYON

Treasures discovered at Chaco Canyon

Archaeology students recently made some amazing discoveries on a **dig** in the Chaco Canyon area of New Mexico.

"They are fascinating discoveries," said the professor in charge of the dig. "We've uncovered beautiful pottery and shells in the ruins of a house that's 1,000 years old!" The professor explained that they examined the wood used to build the house. He said that tests showed that the wood was 1,000 years old.

The professor and his students found pieces of pottery decorated with black patterns on a white background. This was the **traditional** colour used by the Ancestral Puebloans, the people who lived there. Pieces of red-on-black pottery were also found. "This pottery would have come from another area," said one of the students. "This shows that the people who lived here traded with other people. The shells were from a coastal area so they would also have been traded."

"With a piece of pottery, we can tell how old it is, and where it comes from by its shape, the material it is made from, and the patterns of decorations."

"Pottery, tools and rock art give us important clues about the past," said the professor. "Tools can tell us what kind of work people did and whether they were hunters or farmers," said another student. "That gives us a clue to what they might have eaten."

A piece of traditional Anasazi pottery, probably used for storing food or liquid

"Sometimes, scientists work together to solve the puzzles of the past," said the professor. "I remember one dig when we found some animal remains. We got a **palaeontologist** to identify what kind of animal the bones were from. She also found some plant pollen **fossils**, and that gave us another solution to the puzzle of what the people who had lived in the area ate. Sometimes, it's just like being a detective."

An example of red-on-black pottery found in the Chaco Canyon area

Ancient Australian canyon

At Kings Canyon in the Northern Territory, Aboriginal Watarrka Rangers have helped palaeontologists with locating fossilised tracks of ancient marine creatures in sandstone rock deposited about 400 million years ago. These fossils in the 100-metre rock walls of the canyon gorge tell scientists about when life first appeared on land and the geological changes that have taken place over time.

Chapter 6

Time detectives of the future

A time capsule is a small collection of objects from a particular time and place that make up a snapshot of life. A time capsule that was made 100 years ago has been stored at City Hall and will be opened on 1 January.

Make your own time capsule

Scientists are always discovering new ways of finding out about the past. You can help scientists of the future understand the people of the 21st century. What would you choose?

What you need

- A time capsule
- A selection of things to include in the capsule

What you do

1. Place the chosen objects inside the capsule.
2. Seal the capsule.
3. Ask permission to bury the capsule in your yard. Don't forget the spot where you buried your capsule. You can look at it in ten years. What do you think will have changed?

Discoveries around the world

Can you find these places in an atlas?

East Africa

The Rift Valley is believed to be the first place in the world where humans lived. **Archaeologists** and other experts have studied human **fossils** from this area that are more than three million years old.

Australia

Lake Mungo is where the oldest human bones in Australia have been found. Tests on the human fossils prove that Aboriginal people lived in the area around 40,000 years ago. Archaeologists discovered tools that show the Aboriginal people were among the first people to grind flour.

China

In 1974, archaeologists discovered over 8,000 life-size terracotta statues of warriors and horses that are more than 2,200 years old. It is an important find because it shows the clothes and weapons of a Chinese army from that **era**.

England

Stonehenge is a ring of large standing stones about 4,000 years old. Archaeologists have not yet solved the puzzle of what Stonehenge was used for. Perhaps it was a temple, a burial site for important people or a place to study the night sky.

Peru

Machu Picchu or the "Lost City of the Incas" is high in the Andes Mountains in a beautiful tropical forest. Archaeologists know it was built around 600 years ago, but the puzzle of when and why the Incas suddenly left the city remains unsolved.

Glossary

algebra	a type of maths that uses symbols to represent numbers
ancient	long ago, in the early time of human history
archaeologists	people who study people and events from the past
architecture	buildings
civilisation	the highly developed way of life of a group of people, including their science, art and government
debris	what is left when something has been destroyed
decomposed	rotted
dig	a place that is being dug up to be studied by archaeologists
era	a period of time in history
excavating	digging carefully in the hope of discovering items of interest or importance from the past
fossils	the remains or imprints (such as a skeleton or footprint) of animals or plants that lived long ago
geometry	a type of maths used to figure out how big a space is
nomads	people who move from place to place
obelisks	tall, four-sided stones, narrower at the top than at the bottom; in ancient times their shadows were used to tell the time
palaeontologists	people who study fossils
papyrus	a plant that grows in water and was used by ancient Egyptians to make paper, rope and other materials
pilgrimages	long journeys to a special place
prehistoric	the time before people recorded history or wrote down what was happening in the world
Roman	a person living during the time of ancient Rome
sundials	devices that show the time by the position of a shadow
tombs	structures where someone is buried
traditional	the ways of doing things that a group of people pass on to their children, who then pass them on to their children, and so on

Index